THE TREASURY
OF ESZTERGOM CATHEDRAL

D0897108

Pál Cséfalvay

The Treasury
of Esztergom
Cathedral

Corvina Kiadó

Title of the original: Az esztergomi főszékesegyházi kincstár
Corvina Kiadó, Budapest, 1984
Translated by Elizabeth Hoch
Translation revised by Margaret Davies
Photographs by Attila Mudrák and Károly Szelényi
Design by Mária Keleti

On the cover: Corvinus Drinking Horn, *c.* 1480

On the back of cover: The Báthori Chasuble (detail), *c.* 1520

© Pál Cséfalvay, 1984

ISBN 963 13 1691 1

Printed in Hungary, 1984
Zrínyi Printing House, Budapest
CO 2295-h-8488

Introduction

Ecclesiastical treasuries originally consisted of collections of valuable objects: chalices, crosses, monstrances, reliquaries, chasubles, etc. which were used for divine services.

The treasuries of cathedrals, being under the rule of a bishop, archbishop or the primate himself, have always contained objects of outstanding artistic and intrinsic value. They were stored in individually locked small, secure strong-rooms, and were used only on major occasions.

The cathedral in Esztergom is the metropolitan church of the Primate of Hungary. Although only a fraction of its treasures have survived, it is still the richest ecclesiastical repository in the country. The original collection, especially the objects dating from the Middle Ages, was greatly depleted by repeated sackings, attempts to save them from Napoleon, and compulsory confiscation in time of war. The treasures of the Cathedral's Treasury have had to be removed to different places thirteen times, which has been particularly detrimental to the religious vestments.

The idea of presenting the religious material in the form of a museum matured at the end of the nineteenth century. The Treasury was developed and made accessible to the public by Prince Primate János Simor (†1891), the great builder and founder of museums, in 1886. He was impelled in this endeavour above all by aesthetic and scholarly considerations, but his desire to

5

re-establish the earlier splendour and greatness of his See also played an important role. To this end he endeavoured to enrich the existing collections by a policy of discriminating purchases, so that both traditional and contemporary trends of art should be represented in the collection. He also spent large sums on the restoration of the existing medieval objects.

In the 1930s Canon Antal Lepold (†1971) transformed the Treasury into a balanced exhibition of stylistic evolution by completing the earlier material through purchases and the inclusion of pieces that were acquired from the Ipolyi Collection. The Treasury is still being enriched by gifts and bequests.

Chronologically, the artefacts now in the Treasury include a Carolingian crystal cross, eight pieces of Romanesque goldsmith's work, a tapestry and four pieces of work by fourteenth-century goldsmiths, twenty-two textile pieces, and twenty-seven pieces of goldsmith's work from the late Gothic or Renaissance periods. The number of the Baroque and nineteenth-century works of art is so large that only selected pieces of these periods can be displayed.

The first inventory of the Treasury dates from 1528. Its first systematic elaboration was published by the Prelate Franz Bock in Vienna in 1859. Countless books, articles, reviews and guides have appeared since, both on individual pieces in the collection and on the Treasury as a whole.

The latest scientific inventory of the works in precious metals was drawn up by Éva Kovács, that of the textiles by Mária Csernyánszky, both in 1964. I am indebted to both authors for the more recent results they have kindly made available to me.

Bibliography

Dankó, József: **Történelmi, műirodalmi és okmánytári részletek az esztergomi főegyház kincstárából** [The Treasury of the Cathedral at Esztergom. Historical, literary and archival details]. Esztergom, 1880.

Gerevich, Tibor: **Esztergomi műkincsek. Prímás album** [Works of art from Esztergom. The primate's album]. Budapest, 1928, pp. 179–263.

Lepold, Antal: **Adatok az esztergomi főszékesegyházi kincstár történetéhez** [Particulars of the history of the Treasury of Esztergom Cathedral]. Esztergom, 1929.

Csernyánszky, Mária: **Az esztergomi főszékesegyházi kincstár paramentumai** [Religious vestments in the Treasury of the Cathedral at Esztergom]. Budapest, 1933.

Genthon, István: **Az esztergomi főszékesegyházi kincstár** [The Treasury of the Cathedral at Esztergom]. Budapest, 1938.

Lepold, Antal: **Az esztergomi főszékesegyházi kincstár katalógusa** [Catalogue of the Treasury of the Cathedral at Esztergom]. Budapest, 1942.

Gerevich, Tibor (ed.): **Magyarország műemléki topográfiája** [The topography of historical monuments in Hungary]. Vol. I. **Esztergom Műemlékei.** Part I. Compiled by István Genthon. Budapest, 1948, pp. 217–286.

Somogyi, Árpád: **Az esztergomi kincstár** [The Treasury in Esztergom]. Budapest, 1967.

Description of the Objects

1 Rock-crystal with Calvary Scene

Lorraine (Metz); *c.* 870
Inv. No.: 1964.1.1.
6.4 × 4.9 cm.

A deeply convex domed oval crystal with engravings of Christ on the Cross, the Virgin Mary and St. John the Apostle on its flat polished reverse, the sun, the moon at the top, and a dragon at the foot of the Cross. Only about half a dozen similar crystals exist.
It is the oldest piece in the Treasury.

2 Byzantine Icon Reliquary (Staurotheca)

Byzantine, end of
12th–early 13th century
(as determined by Éva
Kovács)
Inv. No.: 1964.3.1.
Silver-gilt; 35 × 25 cm.

Silver-gilt plate on a wooden core covered with oriental silk, embellished with representations in gold cloisonné enamel arranged in three rows. At the intersection point of the ebony cross in the centre of the panel there was once a relic from the Holy Cross. Above, the half-length figures of two mourning angels. In the middle, Constantine the Great and St. Helena. The lower row of pictures shows the rarely depicted scene of Christ being led to the cross and the Descent from the Cross. Among the arabesque patterns decorating the contemporary frame of embossed metal are shown the figures of the most venerated saints of the Eastern Church: St. Basil, St. Nicholas, St. Demetrius and St. Theodore.
The reliquary came to the Treasury from the estate of Archbishop János Kutassy (†1601).

3 Coronation Oath Cross

Hungarian, second third
of 13th century
Inv. No.: 1964.4.1.
Gold; height: 40.2 cm.

Standing cross with arms terminating in seven lobes. The front is richly decorated with tendrils in filigree work, precious stones and pearls. The reverse side is also embellished with filigree. Cardinal Péter Pázmány (†1637) had the cross restored in 1634. It was on this occasion that the four-lobed front and back plaques, the representation of Our Lady of Hungary were added, and the pedestal was made by using three of the original plaques of filigree work.
The upper part of the cross is an outstanding piece of medieval Hungarian goldsmith's work.
After the seventeenth century the cross was used at the ceremony of coronation.

4 Medieval Liturgical Objects

Reliquary casket
(Inv. No.: 1964.7.1.);
candlestick
(Inv. No.: 1964.9.1.);
pyx (Inv. No.: 1964.10.1.);
corpus from a processional cross
(Inv. No.: 1964.8.1.).
Limoges, *c*. 1250
Copper with traces
of gilding and champlevé
enamel

When in 1241–42 the Mongols devastated Hungary, they also ransacked the churches. The liturgical objects thus lost were replaced mainly by pieces of fine metalwork from Limoges (France) where their production had developed on a commercial basis.
From the Arnold Ipolyi Collection.

5 Figure of Christ from Esztergom

Hungarian, second half
of 12th century
Inv. No.: 1964.6.1.
Gilded cast bronze;
height: 8.7 cm.

Found in 1937 among the ruins of the medieval royal castle at Esztergom.
From a processional cross or an altar cross. Right hand and both legs broken.

6 Processional Cross

Limoges, *c.* 1250
Inv. No.: 1964.5.1.
Copper-gilt on wooden
core; height: 58.3 cm.

On the front of the cross the figure of
Christ and saints adorned with
champlevé enamel and artificial gems.
Enamelled plaquettes cover the reverse.
The cross was found in the outskirts of
the town of Szarvas (Békés County) in
1942. Canon Antal Lepold (†1971) had it
restored. Later he donated it to the
Treasury.

7 Chalice

Italian, *c.* 1350
Inv. No.: 1964.13.1.
Copper-gilt; its more recent
cup is silver-gilt;
height: 18 cm.

The six-lobed foot and stem are
enamelled. The knop is adorned with six
small pictures of translucent enamel.
Purchased by Primate János Simor from
the Cologne Schnütgen Collection in
1884.

8 István Baráti's Standing Cross

Italian, *c.* 1380,
with later additions.
(According to Hans R.
Hahnloser,
the work of Bertusius
whose similar cross is
in the custody of Sta Croce
in Florence)
Inv. No.: 1964.16.1.
Silver-gilt with rock-crystal
plates;
height: 92 cm.

Garnet-decorated rock-crystal plates in
lily-shaped setting. In the centre of the
cross is a reliquary surrounded by small
Gothic niches. The Corpus Christi, the
inscription INRI, the garnet decoration
and the coat of arms of the donor were
added in 1607.
A gift of István Baráti, land-steward of
the Primate, presented to the Cathedral
in 1607.

9 Crystal Reliquary

French, *c.* 1380
Inv. No.: 1964.30.1.
Rock-crystal in silver-gilt
frame; height: 13.5 cm.

This small rock-crystal vessel, originally
a salt-cellar, stands on a stem and has
a cover. The stem represents a tree-trunk
under which a ragged gnome-like figure

is seen on a green enamel terrace. He has a cask and staff, and is surrounded by a dog, a goat and three lambs. The top of the crystal lid is decorated with a bunch of flowers in blue enamel, and the rim with rubies.
Donated to the Treasury by Canon Imre Egri (†1630).

10 Reliquary

Italian, 14th century
Inv. No.: 1964.15.1.
Copper-gilt with glass cup; height: 33 cm.

The six-lobed foot is surmounted by an enamel-decorated knop. The lid bears the Gothic inscription: "Giovanni Emanito Paladini". The cross is a more recent addition.
From the Arnold Ipolyi Collection.

11 Drinking Horn

From the Rhineland or France,
before 1408
Inv. No.: 1964.17.1,2.
The horn of an aurochs in silver-gilt setting; height: 70.5 cm.

The finest surviving piece of its kind, remarkable for its decorative statuettes, niello scenes and coats of arms. It may have served as a centre piece on a princely table. In the Cathedral it was used as a chrismal together with the other horns. It bears the coats of arms of the Palóczy family and Emperor Sigismund of Luxembourg. The mounted figure of St. George and the ornamental lid are nineteenth-century additions.
It is assumed that it was presented to Sigismund by the grand master of the Teutonic Order in 1408. Sigismund must have given it to Archbishop György Palóczy (†1439), from whose estate it found its way to the Treasury.

12 Drinking Horn

From the Rhineland
or France,
before 1408
Inv. No.: 1964.18.1,2
The horn of an aurochs
in silver-gilt setting;
height: 48 cm.

Standing on three gryphon feet. The tip
of the horn is surmounted by a figurine
of St. George. The belt encircling the
middle is decorated with coats of arms:
a one-headed eagle on the one side and
a double-headed eagle on the other.
Above them a plaque depicting St. John
the Baptist and an ornamental addition
to the cover, both of which date from
the nineteenth century.
The provenance of the horn is similar to
that of No. 11.

---

13 Calvary of King Matthias Corvinus

Upper part:
made in Paris, 1402;
pedestal: presumably
Lombard, c. 1469–1490
Inv. No.: 1964.19.1.
Gold, with precious
stones and pearls;
height: 72.5 cm.

The calvary is one of the principal pieces
in the Cathedral's Treasury. The
figurines are covered with a special
ronde-bosse gold enamel. The upper part
is characteristically Gothic: it depicts the
Crucifixion, below which the figure of
Christ tied to a column appears in
a niche, with three prophets. As
established by Éva Kovács, this part was
executed in response to a commission
from the wife of Philip the Bold, Duke
of Burgundy, as a New Year's present
for her husband in 1403. The piece is an
outstanding example of a goldsmith's
work from the Parisian court.
As testified to the coat of arms, its lower
part must have been made in the time of
King Matthias Corvinus, and is probably
the work of a master trained in
Lombardy. It is decorated with sphinxes,
dolphins, mythological pictures in
enamel and the coat of arms of the king.
According to a document, János
Corvinus (†1504), the natural son of
King Matthias, first put the calvary in
pawn with Archbishop Tamás Bakócz,
and in 1494 he definitely transferred it to
him.

14 Corvinus Drinking Horn

Hungarian, c. 1480
Inv. No.: 1964.29.1,2.
The horn of an aurochs
in silver-gilt setting;
height: 50 cm.

Standing on three gryphon feet. The belt is decorated with a dragon. Its tip is surmounted by a small Gothic fort with towers. The figure of St. George on the top is a nineteenth-century addition. The horn was donated to the Cathedral by János Corvinus.

15 Benedek Suki's Chalice

Hungarian, c. 1440
Inv. No.: 1964.21.1,2.
Silver-gilt; height: 27 cm.

The most beautiful Hungarian Late Gothic chalice, decorated with a multitude of cast figurines, engraved scenes from the Bible and extremely fine filigree enamel. In a field of the pedestal the coat of arms of the Suki family, the head of a wolf standing out of a crown, can be seen.
According to the inscription on the casing of the cup, the chalice is the gift of "bnedictus de Swk" and was probably executed for the cathedral in Gyulafehérvár (now Alba Iulia, Rumania).

16 Rock-crystal Casket

From the Netherlands
or Upper Italy, c. 1450
Inv. No.: 1964.46.1.
Cut rock-crystal plaques
on a silver base; height:
29 cm, length: 43 cm.

Translucent silver-enamel with vitrified decorative motifs. Originally a jewel-case, it was a characteristic piece of court art. An exceptionally large rock-crystal work of art.

17 Cardinal Dénes Széchy's Chalice

Hungarian, c. 1450
Inv. No.: 1964.23.1,2.
Silver-gilt; height: 23.5 cm.

The pedestal and the cup-casing are decorated alternately with fields of filigree enamel and filigree work. The stem bears the inscriptions "got hilf" and "maria". On the foot the coat of arms of Cardinal Dénes Széchy (†1465).

18 Chalice from Szakolca

Hungarian, c. 1490
Inv. No.: 1964.28.1,2.
Silver-gilt; height: 22.5 cm.

Its six-lobed foot and cup-casing are decorated with white filigree enamel rosettes on alternating blue and green bases. The knop is embellished with six amethysts set in fields of filigree work. The stem bears the inscription "ihesus" and "o maria".
Primate János Simor purchased the work from St. Michael's Church in Szakolca (now Skalica, Czechoslovakia). He had it restored in 1871.

19 Chalice of Matthias the Literate

Hungarian, c. 1480
Inv. No.: 1964.31.1,2.
Silver-gilt; height: 23 cm.

Its six-lobed pedestal, knop and frieze-edged cup-casing are covered with a fine network of filigree work consisting of a circle of rosettes. The filigree is decorated with a great many tiny golden granules. The stem bears the inscription "MATHIE LITERATI".

20 Chalice from Garamszentbenedek

Hungarian, c. 1480
Inv. No.: 1964.32.1,2.
Silver-gilt; height: 22.4 cm.

The six-lobed foot, the knop and the cup-casing are decorated with filigree work. The goldsmith has used smaller and larger granules and strawberry-shaped ornaments to enrich the design. The cup was made at a later date. Garamszentbenedek is now Hronský Beňadik in Czechoslovakia.

21 Large Filigree Chalice

Transylvanian, c. 1480
Inv. No.: 1964.33.1,2.
Silver-gilt, height: 26.5 cm.

Decorated with extremely fine filigree work. On the six-lobed foot the centre of each filigree field is ornamented with granulation. Red and blue precious

stones embellish the knop. The cup was
made in Vienna in 1856.
From the estate of Canon János
Thomasinovics (†1588).

22 Chalice from Pobedény

Hungarian, c. 1480
Inv. No.: 1964.34.1,2.
Silver-gilt; height: 20.8 cm.

The fields of filigree work are decorated
with silver rosettes, embossed silver
leaves and precious stones.

23 Miklós Oláh's Crosier

Hungarian, c. 1490;
the staff c. 1560
Inv. No.: 1964.35.1,2.
Silver-gilt; height: 188 cm.

The massive head of the crosier is
adorned with precious stones and pearls,
and the Madonna with Child enthroned
on a crescent; above them are two angels
holding a crown. At the back, the sun
appears as a radiating disc. The knop is
formed by a Gothic chapel with niches.
Its scaly staff was made in response to
a commission from Archbishop Miklós
Oláh (†1568) around 1560. The crosier
was used at coronation ceremonies.

24 Corvinus Monstrance

Hungarian,
end of 15th century
Inv. No.: 1964.38.1.
Silver-gilt; height: 67.5 cm.

Tripartite Gothic tower structure with
statuettes of saints in its Gothic niches.
It surrounds the round pyx (lunule) in
which the consecrated holy host is
displayed. A great many pinnacles
decorated with crockets and finials
enrich the design. The pedestal and knop
were executed in response to
a commission from Péter Pázmány
(†1637).
According to recent research, however,
the work was a gift László Rosályi Kun
presented to Cardinal Pázmány from
King Matthias Corvinus's treasury at an
earlier date.

25 Pontifical Pectoral

Hungarian, *c.* 1490
Inv. No.: 1964.37.1.
Silver-gilt;
diameter: 16.5 cm.

Octagonal reliquary decorated with rosettes and precious stones. The inserted mother-of-pearl relief shows the martyrdom of St. Catherine of Alexandria. In the Middle Ages prelates wore this type of pectoral reliquary over their liturgical vestments.

26 Gothic Pectoral Clasp

Nagyszeben
(now Sibiu, Rumania),
c. 1500
Inv. No.: 1964.48.1.
Silver-gilt; diameter: 11 cm.

Decorated with enamelled figurines in small niches and precious stones.

27 Apostolic Cross

Italian, second half
of 15th century
Inv. No.: 1964.39.1,2.
Silver-gilt; height (without staff): 32 cm,
width: 26.1 cm.

The figure of Christ is of silver. The quatrefoil medallions at the extremities contain the following figures: on the top a pelican, on the right St. John the Evangelist, on the left the Virgin Mary, at the bottom St. Mary Magdalen. The reverse is decorated with niello half-length pictures of the Madonna (centre) and the four Evangelists. The staff is adorned with an enamelled knop, commissioned by Primate János Simor in Vienna. The cross was carried at the head of the coronation procession.

28 Ciborium

Hungarian or German,
15th century
Inv. No.: 1964.41.1.
Copper-gilt; height: 41 cm.

Hexagonal ciborium, the sides of which are adorned with graved scenes from the life of Christ. The lid is decorated with crockets and scale-work, surmounted by a double-cast finial of more recent date. The six-lobed foot is adorned with

chased acanthus leaves. The inscription "MARIA" and a cross are visible in the blue enamel of the knop.
The ciborium came to the Treasury from the Ipolyi Collection.

29 László Zeleméry's Standing Cross

Hungarian, 1586
Inv. No.: 1964.50.1.
Silver-gilt; height: 68.7 cm.

The triangular, slightly arched pedestal supports a covered cup, from which emerge a pearl-decorated crucifix and two curved arms surmounted by the figures of the Madonna (on the right) and St. John the Evangelist (on the left). The sphinxes seated on the corners of the pedestal support the cup with their wings and hold the chased coat of arms of the Zeleméry family in their paws. The reverse of the cross and of the two assistant figures is decorated with graved scenes from the Old Testament: the serpent winding itself on the Tree of Life, and Moses with Aaron.

30 Péter Pázmány's Pectoral Cross

Hungarian, 1636
Inv. No.: 1964.63.1.
Gold; height: 13.5 cm,
width: 8.6 cm.

Decorated with black champlevé enamel, pearls and precious stones. The reverse shows the Lamb of God and the instruments of the Passion.

31 Miklós Böjthe's Pectoral Cross

South German (?),
first half of 16th century
Inv. No.: 1964.61.1.
Gold; height: 7.5 cm,
width: 5.3 cm.

The obverse is decorated with diamonds and coloured enamel animal figures: frogs, dogs, lions and horses. The reverse shows peacocks and stags in champlevé enamel.

32 Monstrance from Garamszentbenedek

Hungarian, 1640
Inv. No.: 1964.40.1.
Silver-gilt; height: 73 cm.

Above the round pyx, in a very elaborate late Gothic niche, the figure of the Madonna is visible. It is flanked by the figures of St. Adalbert and St. Nicholas in similar niches.

33 György Szelepcsényi's Chalice

Hungarian or German,
c. 1640
Inv. No.: 1964.66.1,2.
Gold; height: 21.3 cm.

The six-lobed foot is adorned with representations from the Gospel in chased relief, coloured enamel pictures showing the Calvary and the coat of arms of György Szelepcsényi. Rubies and angel heads decorate the knop. The relief work on the cup-casing shows St. Adalbert and symbolic figures of Faith, Hope and Love.
The chalice was given to the Cathedral by Primate György Szelepcsényi (†1685) on the occasion of the coronation of Queen Claudia Felicitas, wife to Leopold I.

34 György Szelepcsényi's Crucifix

South German (?), c. 1600
Inv. No.: 1964.70.1.
Gold; height: 29.5 cm,
width: 12.5 cm.

Masterpiece of early Baroque goldsmith's work. It stands on a four-lobed foot decorated with precious stones, enamelled leaves and putti among scroll ornaments. The coat of arms of Primate Szelepcsényi is a later addition. Precious stones and pearls adorn the stem with the figure of Christ in *ronde-bosse* gold enamel. At the coronation the cross was used as cross of peace.

35 Chalice from Salzburg

Master F, Augsburg, 1680
Inv. No.: 1964.72.1,2.
Silver-gilt; height: 27 cm.

The round foot, pear-shaped knop and the casing of the cup are all richly decorated with red garnet. Fifteen oval-shaped enamelled medallions represent the mysteries of the rosary. Commissioned by Küenburg, Archbishop of Salzburg, the chalice was acquired by Canon János Aradi (†1810). Its counterpart is in Salzburg.

36 György Szelepcsényi's Monstrance

Augsburg; signed I. M;
c. 1690
Inv. No.: 1964.73.1.
Silver-gilt; height: 95 cm.

The pedestal is eight-lobed and oval in shape. An angel standing forms the stem and supports the upper part which is also oval. It incorporates a heart-shaped pyx in which a small angel is holding a lunule for containing the consecrated holy host. The top of the work is adorned with embossed figures: the dove which represents the Holy Ghost, God the Father, Mary and Joseph, and finally the pelican. The pedestal and the upper part are embellished with painted enamel medallions framed by precious stones.

37 László Mikola's Votive Plaque

Sebestyén Hann,
Nagyszeben
(now Sibiu, Rumania),
1700
Inv. No.: 1964.77.1.
Silver; 44.5 × 33.5 cm.

The crucified Christ, with St. Francis Xavier kneeling before him, is visible against a landscape background on the right. Above, on the left, in a sun-disc radiating from the clouds, a dove representing the Holy Ghost; in front of it the abbreviated form of the name of Jesus: IHS is inscribed. On the right the coat of arms of the Mikola family.
At the bottom, the text of a vow. Commissioned by László Mikola of Szamosfalva, a Transylvanian associate judge (†1742).

38 Charles Ambrosius's Chalice

Johann Jacob Vogelhund,
Augsburg, 1717
Inv. No.: 1964.84.1,2.
Silver-gilt; height: 29 cm.

The chalice stands on an almost circular foot and is decorated with embossed scenes framed by pearls and precious stones. On the foot the Condemnation of Christ, the Crowning with Thorns, the Flagellation, the instruments of the Passion, the Virgin Mary, St. Joseph and the Christ Child. On the stem: St. Jerome, St. Ambrose and St. George. On the cup-casing, the Agony in the Garden, Christ before Pilate, and Christ before the High Priest Caiaphas.
This chalice came to the Treasury from the estate of Primate Charles Ambrosius (†1809).

39 Charles Ambrosius's Altar Cruets with Plate

Johann Jacob Vogelhund,
Augsburg, 1717
Inv. No.: 1964.83.1,2,3.
Silver-gilt; the plate:
32.8 × 26.8 cm;
height of cruets: 13.8 cm.

The eight-lobed, oval-shaped plate is decorated with scenes in embossed relief showing the Man of Sorrows, the Mourning Virgin and the Resurrection. In fields decorated with precious stones and pearls, the Scourging of Christ, Christ Bearing the Cross, the Crucifixion and the Entombment can be seen, interspersed with Evangelists.
The cruets are adorned with precious stones, pearls and embossed figures. From the estate of Primate Charles Ambrosius (†1809).

40 Imre Esterházy's Monstrance

Georg Caspar Meichl,
Vienna, 1728
Inv. No.: 1964.88.1.
Silver-gilt; height: 94 cm.

The elaborate oval pedestal shows embossed scenes from the Passion of Christ, and the stem represents St. Michael. The pyx and the lunule ornamented with precious stones, are surrounded by a structure shaped like an altar. Above, a cross, below it the Pietà, on the two sides the figures of King

St. Stephen and St. Emeric can be seen. Below them, between two kneeling angels, the Last Supper is represented in relief. The whole upper part is adorned with various precious stones.
Donated by Primate Imre Esterházy (†1745), in 1729.

41 The Maria Theresa Chalice

Graz, 1732
Inv. No.: 1964.89.1,2.
Silver-gilt;
height: 29.6 cm.

The largest and most ornate Baroque chalice in the Treasury. The rich embossed work is decorated with a great many precious stones and coloured enamel pictures in silver cartouches, showing scenes from the Passion.
Received by Primate Imre Esterházy (†1745) from the Empress Maria Theresa.

42 The Hildesheim Cross

German, c. 1750
Inv. No.: 1964.282.1.
Ivory and ebony;
height: 120 cm,
the Corpus: 44 × 33 cm.

The Baroque ivory Corpus was purchased by Primate János Simor from the Bishop of Hildesheim, Daniel Wilhelm Sommerwerk, in 1875; the ebony cross was then made for it to Simor's commission.

43 Altar Cross

Alajos Giergl, Pest, 1838
Inv. No.: 1964.141.1.
Silver, parcel-gilt;
31 × 20 cm.

Oval foot, vase-shaped knop, trefoil ends on the arms. Stylized ornamentation composed of floral elements, executed in the style fashionable during the First Empire in France.
Commissioned by the Cathedral Chapter.

44 Chalice

Master T D, Vienna, 1859
Inv. No.: 1964.188.1,2.
Silver-gilt;
height: 20.5 cm.

This chalice is shown as an example of the neo-Gothic chalices preserved in the Treasury. Designed by József Lippert, the favourite architect of Primate Simor. The six-lobed, scroll and rosette-adorned fields on the foot, the knop and the fleur-de-lis ornamented cup-casing are all embellished with topaz. According to the inscription on the foot, the chalice was produced from silver unearthed at Vaszar, while the topaz came from the St. Sophia at Constantinople. Commissioned by Primate János Simor while he was still bishop of Győr.

45 János Simor's Chalice

Anders, Vienna, 1876
Inv. No.: 1964.165.1,2.
Gold; height: 27 cm.

The round foot bears Primate Simor's coat of arms in enamel. The knop is vase-shaped. The casing of the cup shows the symbolic figures of Faith, Hope and Love. The whole chalice is adorned with blue and black enamel and a great many precious stones. It is the most beautiful example of a neo-Renaissance chalice in the collection.
Designed by József Lippert in response to a commission from Primate János Simor.

46 Crosier

Károly Zitterbarth,
Budapest, 1886
Inv. No.: 1964.259.1.
Silver-gilt;
height: 189 cm.

The crosier ends in an animal head, and is decorated with the figures of the Virgin and King St. Stephen. The knop bears reliefs of St. Ladislas, St. Emeric, St. Elizabeth and St. Margaret. The work is executed in the so-called "historicizing" style which dominated the work of Hungarian goldsmiths after the

Compromise of 1867. It is richly decorated with precious stones and filigree enamel.
Designed by Lajos Rauscher. Presented to Primate János Simor by the Catholic faithful of Budapest on the occasion of his golden jubilee mass in 1886.

47 Arnold Ipolyi's Crosier

Hungarian, c. 1870
Inv. No.: 1964.173.1.
Copper-gilt;
height: 172 cm.

The crosier shows Arnold Ipolyi kneeling before the Good Shepherd. The head is decorated with Transylvanian coloured floral filigree enamel.
Made on the occasion of Arnold Ipolyi's consecration as bishop of Besztercebánya (now Banská Bystrica, Czechoslovakia).

48 Chalice

Hungarian;
signed M Z, 1897
Inv. No.: 1964.235.1.
Silver-gilt;
height: 25.7 cm.

One of the most characteristic neo-Gothic chalices. It is designated to imitate the Suki chalice. Richly decorated with filigree enamel and pearls. The small niches in its stem contain figurines of the Apostles.
Donated by Canon Ferenc Maszlaghy (†1917), in 1897.

49 Chalice

Antal Megyer-Meyer,
Budapest, 1937
Inv. No.: 1964.255.1,2.
Silver-gilt, ivory; height: 26.5 cm.

The straight ivory stem with engraved ornamentation rises from a circular flat pedestal. The cup is flat at the bottom. The work was commissioned by the Cathedral Chapter on the occasion of the World Eucharistic Congress held in Budapest in 1938.

50 Anjou Wall Hanging (Antependium?)

Hungarian embroidery
on Italian velvet, *c.* 1370
Inv. No.: 1964.317.
128 × 274 cm.

Embroidery with coloured silk, gold and silver threads on red velvet. In the centre, Christ rising from His tomb, surrounded by stars; on top, Anjou coats of arms, the apostolic cross alternating with fleurs-de-lis; on the two sides ornamental foliate pattern of later date. The work is said to originate from Göncruszka (Borsod-Abaúj-Zemplén County).
Acquired by purchase from art dealers by Canon Antal Lepold, who donated it to the Treasury in 1941.

51 Lenten Embroidery

Hungarian (?), *c.* 1500
Inv. No.: 1964.316.
125 × 186 cm.

Partly embroidered cloth appliqué on twentieth-century black velvet background representing Christ on the Cross with angels holding the instruments of the Passion. According to Mária Csernyánszky, the figure of Christ is an addition made at a later date.
From the Lajos Némethy Collection.

52 Coronation Mitre

Hungarian, *c.* 1430
Inv. No.: 1964.318.
37 × 35 cm.

The white silk base is fully covered by rich bead-work. The mitre is framed and divided into fields by spiral borders. Thirty-four precious stones (cabochons) are set into its surface. The bands are suspended by silver-gilt hinges ornamented with parrots and leaves.
From the period of Primate György Pálóczi (†1439).

53 a–b Embroidered Altar for Private Devotion (Diptych)

Hungarian, *c.* 1500
Inv. No.: 1964.314.1,2.
20.7 × 18.5 cm each

Two more recent wooden boxes covered on the outside with red silk; the inside is lined with golden cloth. The box on the left contains a head of Christ with the Crown of Thorns; that on the right, the Mater Dolorosa. The raised embroidery is executed with coloured silk and gold thread over a wooden core and decorated with pearls.
The origin of the altar is unknown, but the item is recorded as early as in the inventory of 1609.

54 Violet Chasuble

Italian gold brocade
with Hungarian
embroidery, *c.* 1500
Inv. No.: 1964.309.
140 × 104 cm.

The design of the brocade is composed of pineapple-shaped palmettes bordered by scrolls, which form pointed oval fields on the violet silk base. The cross's unified composition shows Flemish influence: its raised embroidery stands out against a gold base with geometric patterns. Above, the Virgin is kneeling between God the Father and God the Son; below, three angels are carrying her towards heaven. Still lower the Apostles are surrounding the Virgin's open grave, while at the bottom the kneeling figure of St. Thomas is lifting his hands. The chasuble has survived without any alteration in its original size and form.

55 The Kutassy Chasuble

Hungarian embroidery
on Italian brocade, *c.* 1500
Inv. No.: 1964.299.
129 × 75 cm.

Yellow silk brocade with silver loops and pomegranate pattern. On the cross are figures of Hungarian saints. In the domed niche supported by twisted columns, the full-length figures of the Blessed Virgin, St. Stephen, St. Ladislas and St. Emeric, and on the arms of the

cross the half-length figures of
St. Augustine and St. Jerome can be
seen.
In 1590 Primate Kutassy (†1601) had his
personal coat of arms embroidered on
the garment.

56 Chasuble with Tree

Hungarian embroidery,
second half of 15th century
Inv. No.: 1964.295.
110 cm.

On new red velvet, embroidery with
Christ on the Cross, the latter depicted
as a tree without foliage. Below, in the
niche, the embroidered figure of
St. Ursula.
From the Lajos Némethy Collection.

57 Chasuble

Hungarian raised
embroidery
on Italian velvet brocade,
15th century
Inv. No.: 1964.307.
131 × 81 cm.

Pineapple design surrounded by
pomegranate flowers outlined on red
velvet on a gold base. The crowned
Madonna is flanked by two floating
angels. Below, St. Catherine of
Alexandria and St. Dorothy.
Preserved in its original length.

58 The Széchy Chasuble

Hungarian embroidery
on Italian velvet brocade,
c. 1480
Inv. No.: 1964.303.
128 × 80 cm.

Pineapple pattern on a red velvet base,
worked with gold. On the cross, in
pearl-decorated niches, figures in raised
embroidery. Above, God the Father with
the dove of the Holy Ghost, Christ on
the Cross with angels (the Holy Trinity);
below, St. Mary Magdalen; still lower,
a bishop with a crosier and a book
inscribed "MIT GOTT" (with God); at
the bottom St. George with the dragon
and an unknown coat of arms of a later
date.

59 The Matthias Chasuble

Hungarian embroidery
on Florentine velvet
brocade, *c.* 1500
Inv. No.: 1964.308.
139 × 83.5 cm.

A bunch of palm-leaves and ears of corn
sprout from a red vase surrounded by
a triple feathered garland. Raised
embroidery in coloured silk; figures in
golden and pearl-embroidered garments
in small Gothic niches. Above, the
Madonna; on the arms of the cross, the
half-length figures of St. Francis of
Assisi and St. Louis of Toulouse, below
in niches St. Catherine, St. Dorothy and
St. Anne holding the Virgin and Child.
Some of the ornamental elements and
weaving of the velvet ground has
affinities with the throne hangings of
King Matthias Corvinus.

60 Red Chasuble

Venetian embroidery
on Italian velvet brocade,
c. 1480
Inv. No.: 1964.298.
125 × 75 cm.

Large rosettes spring from a branch with
trifoliate leaves against a base interlaced
with gold. The cross is decorated with
saints in three-domed niches. Above,
St. John the Baptist; below him,
St. Paul, St. Bartholomew and
St. Augustine. On the arms of the cross:
the Annunciation.

61 Green Chasuble

Hungarian raised
embroidery
on Italian velvet brocade,
end of 15th century
Inv. No.: 1964.304.
125 × 76 cm.

The green velvet brocade shows a rich
design of palm-leaves, foliate scrolls and
pomegranates. In the centre, on a gold
latticed base, Christ on the Cross. Above
Him, God the Father; below, the Virgin
and St. John the Evangelist. At the
bottom: St. Mary Magdalen on her
knees embraces the Cross. At the ends of
the horizontal bar St. Peter (left) and
St. Paul (right).

62 Cope from Cologne

Italian velvet
with Rhineland embroidery
showing Flemish influence,
second half of 15th century
Inv. No.: 1964.300.
Length: 141 cm.

Lobed palmette design indicated by omission from the red velvet ground, embellished with pomegranate and pineapple pattern. On the front of the cope two strips of Burgundian embroidery showing strong Flemish influence, with scenes from the life of the Virgin and the Infant Christ. In a shield on the cope's rear side, the Virgin and Child, and above them angels holding a crown are shown on a Cyprian gold base. It is a South German work. The strap bearing a coat of arms is of a later date.
Purchased by Primate Simor from the Cologne Schnütgen Collection in 1884.

---

63 The Báthori Chasuble

Hungarian raised
embroidery
on Florentine brocade,
c. 1520
Inv. No.: 1964.310.
130 × 89 cm.

The thistle-flower and pomegranate design on a gold ground is made of knitted gold threads with red trimming. The surface of the cross is filled with figures of saints in Gothic niches embroidered with pearls and gold thread on a gold base of geometric design. Above, angels are holding a crown over the head of the Madonna who is standing on a crescent. On the right, the half-length figure of St. Margaret with the dragon; on the left, St. Dorothy with flowers. Below them, St. Catherine with the wheel and St. Barbara with the chalice. At the bottom, a double heraldic shield surrounded by dragons, showing the coats of arms of Palatine István Báthori and his wife, the Polish princess Sofia of Mazovia.
The chasuble came to the Cathedral Treasury from the Premonstratensian provostal church in Ipolyság (now Šahy, Czechoslovakia). It is recorded as early as in the inventory of 1609.

64 Mitre

Hungarian,
end of 16th century
Inv. No.: 1964.319.
37 × 33 cm.

Decorated with a design of rosettes and acanthus leaves in rich bead-work on a scarlet velvet base of recent date. The rosettes each have a precious stone in the centre. The baluster-shaped metal tassels at the end of the ribbons are of special interest. Thoroughly restored in the nineteenth century. In former times it was used to decorate the statue of St. Adalbert on the saint's feast-day.

65 The Bakócz Chasuble

Italian embroidery
on Spanish brocatelle,
c. 1510
Inv. No.: 1964.311.
104 × 78 cm.

On a ground of red silk interlaced with extremely fine gilt wire, the design of artichokes appears surrounded by palmettes and foliage in a double frame. The cross is bordered by a wide stripe of gold embroidery. The six round medallions among Renaissance-style brackets and meandering acanthus scrolls are half-length figures embroidered with metal and silk threads. On top St. Peter, below him St. Philip and St. James the Less. At the bottom, the coat of arms of Cardinal Bakócz. The arms of the cross show the Annunciation. St. Thomas the Apostle was put in its present place at a later date.
According to Tibor Gerevich, the embroidery was based on a design by Pinturicchio.

66 The Thurzó Passion-shield

Hungarian embroidery
with pearls, 1597
Inv. No.: 1964.315.
54.4 × 42.6 cm.

On a red silk base decorated with network the symbols of the four Evangelists are shown. The heraldic shield in the centre bearing three helmets is divided by pearls into sixteen fields containing the symbols and instruments of the Passion. Above the shield a small red processional flag; below it, the inscription commemorating the donation.

Originally a gift of Szaniszló Thurzó of Betlenfalva, Count of Szepes (†1625), to Primate Kutassy on the occasion of his inauguration in 1597.

67 The Pázmány Chasuble

Hungarian, beginning
of 17th century
Inv. No.: 1964.323.1,2.
102 × 76 cm.

The relatively new pink taffeta base is divided by silver braid vertically into three fields containing sumptuous coloured Renaissance flower ornaments. At the bottom of the central field is the coat of arms of Cardinal Péter Pázmány (†1637).

68 Coronation Chasuble

Hungarian pearl
embroidery,
second half of 17th century
Inv. No.: 1964.329.1–7.
97 × 75 cm.

On a relatively new gold base three vertical fields with Hungarian so-called genteel embroidery motifs; the central field has cut amethysts.

Said to have been commissioned by Primate György Szelepcsényi.

69 Chasuble

Hungarian, early 18th
century
Inv. No.: 1964.331.1–6.
104 cm.

Stylized Baroque flower motifs in three rows on a relatively new silk base. One of the most beautiful embroideries of the Treasury.

70 Brussels Lace

Brussels, c. 1700
Inv. No.: 1964.366.
Width: 64 cm.

The oldest among the many beautiful pieces of lace in the custody of the Treasury. It is embellished with profane subjects, such as sprinkling and dancing women, and stylized flower motifs.

2

4

5

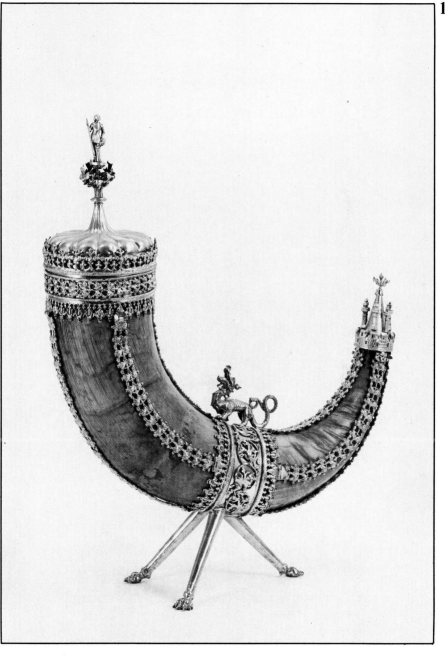

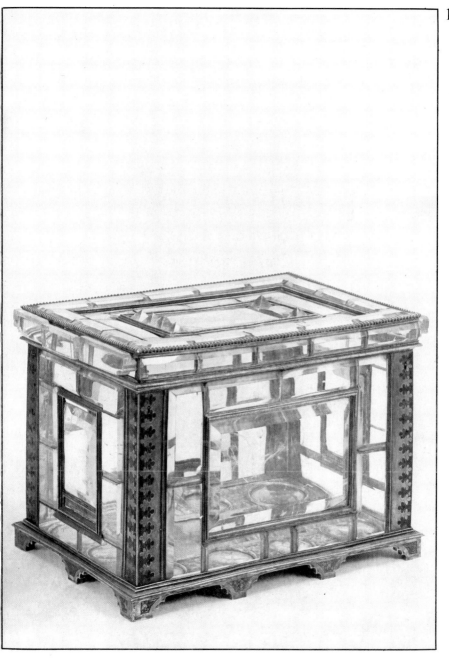

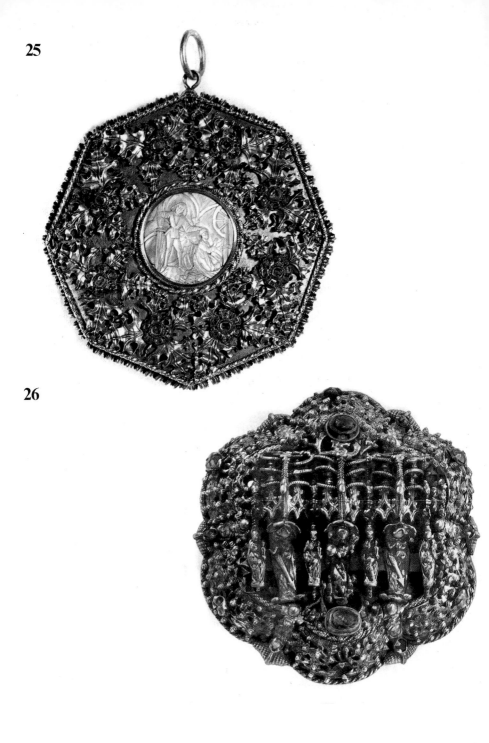

25

26

30

31

33

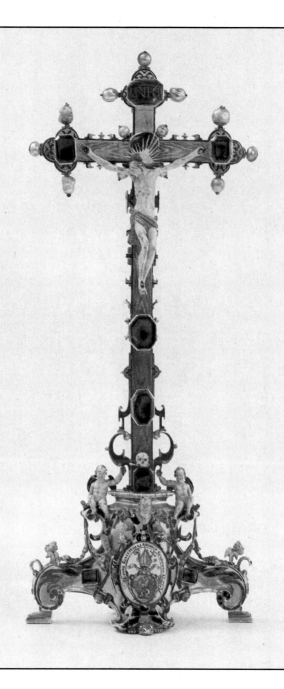

S. FRANCISCVS XAVERIVS. S.I.
INDIARVM II. IAPONIARVM I. APOSTOLVS CVIVS HONORI HANC IMAGINEM
ARGENTEAM CVRAVIT EX VOTO LADISLAVS MIKOLA DE S. AMOS FALVA A 700

39

42

43

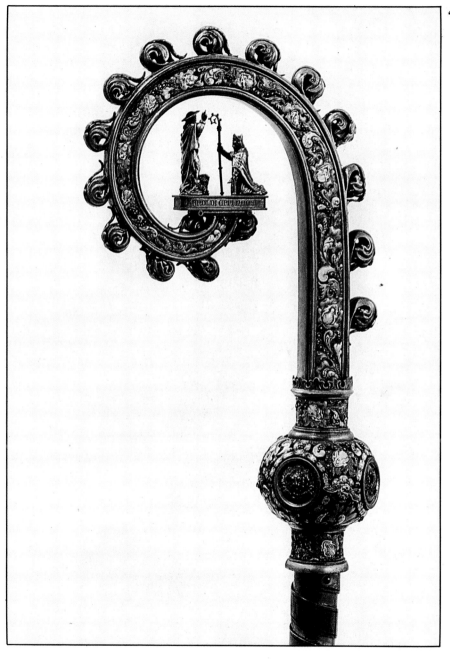

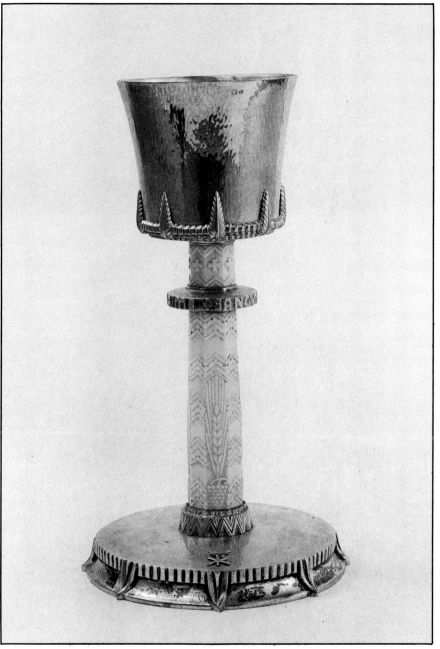

50

51

53a

53b